Guide to Owning a Bull Terrier

Muriel P. Lee

Contents

Distributed in the UNITED STATES to the Pet Trade by T.F.H. Publications, Inc., One T.F.H. Plaza, Neptune City, NJ 07753; on the Internet at www.tfh.com; in CANADA Rolf C. Hagen Inc., 3225 Sartelon St. Laurent-Montreal Quebec H4R 1E8; Pet Trade by H & L Pet Supplies Inc., 27 Kingston Crescent, Kitchener, Ontario N2B 2T6; in ENGLAND by T.F.H. Publications, PO Box 15, Waterlooville PO7 6BQ; in AUSTRALIA AND THE SOUTH PACIFIC by T.F.H. (Australia), Pty. Ltd., Box 149, Brookvale 2100 N.S.W., Australia; in NEW ZEALAND by Brooklands Aquarium Ltd. 5 McGiven Drive, New Plymouth, RD1 New Zealand; in SOUTH AFRICA, Rolf C. Hagen S.A. (PTY.) LTD. P.O. Box 201199, Durban North 4016, South Africa; in Japan by T.F.H. Publications, Japan—Jiro Tsuda, 10-12-3 Ohjidai, Sakura, Chiba 285, Japan. Published by T.F.H. Publications, Inc.

MANUFACTURED IN THE
UNITED STATES OF AMERICA
BY T.F.H. PUBLICATIONS, INC.

INTRODUCTION TO THE BULL TERRIER

Is it a white Cavalier? Is it a kid in a dog suit? Or is it Spuds, the beer promoter? He has been called all of these names, but he is officially known as the Bull Terrier. There is the White Bull Terrier and there is the Colored Bull Terrier. In addition, there is the Miniature Bull Terrier that comes in both colors.

Is he a gentleman? Of course, even if he originally worked in the pits as a fighting dog. Is he fun and full of personality? Yes, or he wouldn't be promoting beer or acting like a kid! Although his original instincts are not completely lost to him, he is now most at home while entertaining and loving his family. This strong, sturdy dog may not be for everyone, but if you like a robust, alert, and very bright animal, this may just be the breed for you.

Dr. Dieter Fleig wrote in his book, *Bull Terriers*: "Bull Terriers are dogs for happy people who enjoy a hearty joke and are able to smile from ear to ear about themselves and their dogs."

The Bull Terrier is well known for his steady temperament, powerful build, and legendary courage.

HISTORY OF THE BULL TERRIER

The Bull Terrier is one of the oldest breeds and is classified in the Terrier Group. The breed traces its origin back to the early 1800s, and it is one of the oldest breeds recognized by the American Kennel Club.

The Bull Terrier belongs to the group of dogs described as terriers, from the Latin word *terra*, meaning earth. The terrier is a dog that has been bred to work beneath the ground to drive out large and small vermin, rodents, and other animals that can be a nuisance to country living. However, the Bull Terrier has a different purpose than the go-to-ground dogs, having been originally bred as a fighting dog. Of the 25 dogs in the Terrier Group, the American Staffordshire Terrier, the Bull Terrier, the Miniature Bull Terrier, and the Staffordshire Bull Terrier were all developed as dogs to work the pits and to entertain spectators by competing in the inhumane sport of dog fighting. Although these breeds are descended from Mastiffs and Bulldogs, they were interbred with terriers to enhance their agility and intelligence. As breeding

Throughout the years, dedicated breeders have devoted themselves to the welfare and development of the Bull Terrier.

Once a fighting dog, the Colored Bull Terrier possesses the same virtues as his white-colored cousins.

progressed, these fighting dogs became sleeker and more streamlined—less "bully" and more terrier—thus, their placement in the Terrier Group.

All of the dogs in the Terrier Group originated in the British Isles, with the exception of the Miniature Schnauzer (Germany). Terriers, although they may differ in type, all have the same character, being game dogs who are agile, tough, smart, and make good companions for their masters. As early as 1735, *The Sportsman's Dictionary* described the Terriers as "a kind of hound, used only or chiefly for hunting the fox or badger. He creeps into the ground and then nips and bites the fox and badger, either by tearing them in pieces with his

teeth, or else hauling them and pulling them by force out of their lurking holes."

From the terriers' earliest beginnings, they were tough, fearless animals who were smart enough to outfox the prey that they were after. It was a natural choice to breed the larger, slower fighting dogs with the smaller, sleeker game terrier.

To have an understanding of the history of the Bull Terrier, there must be some knowledge of the British Isles in the 1700s and early 1800s. The times were hard, the general populace was poor, and cruelty to animals was as common as cruelty to one another. Dog fighting, with its prior background of badger, bull, and bear baiting, was not outlawed in England until 1835. Until then, dog fighting (and previously, bullbaiting) was one of the more popular sports of the common people and at that time, little or no concern was given to the cruelty of the sport. Living conditions were tough, and people, by and large, were uneducated. Dog fighting provided entertainment that was cheap and exciting, in addition to offering the spectators an opportunity to place their bets on the side.

Picture the dogs pitted one against another in a pit, similar to a boxing ring, with the raucous spectators pressed up against the pit, urging their favorite animal to get the better of his opponent. Amid the clamor and noise (and smells, as one can imagine), money is passing hands as the dogs are ready to fight to the death. Not a pretty picture.

The origins of the Bull Terrier are fairly clear compared to some of the other terrier breeds whose backgrounds are still open for speculation. The Bulldog, descended from the old Mastiff, was used for baiting bulls and badgers and eventually for dog fighting. The Bulldog was crossed with various terriers to add a ferocity and tenacity to the Bulldog's strength and courage. The famed dog writer, Stonehenge, wrote of these crosses: "Such a dog to be useful, must be more than half terrier or he will be too heavy and slow,

The pure milk-white Bull Terrier originated in the 1850s in Birmingham, England.

have too much underjaw to hold well with his teeth, and too little command to obey the orders of his master."

With this addition of the terrier, the fighting dog became higher in leg, longer in head, and acquired the terrier fire. These early dogs were called Bull and Terriers. The dogs were unattractive, with blocky heads, and were of all colors, including white. They were bred for the purpose of fighting rather than for their looks. Those who were unable to do the job were destroyed, and those who could do the proper work were bred one to another with little regard for type.

"Unless they were fit and game for the purpose, their heads were not kept long out of the huge butt of water in the stable yard," Stonehenge wrote. Worse yet, for those who were not agile, tenacious, or quick, life was cut short in the pit.

In the 1850s, James Hinks, of Birmingham, who was considered the father of the breed, outcrossed his dog to the now extinct White English Terrier, a sleek, stylish-looking dog. (It is also noted that Hinks had some crosses to the Dalmatian and possibly the Greyhound and Foxhound.) In 1862, he introduced his pure white strain of the Bull Terrier at a dog show. His dog was not only white in color but showed a refinement and grace that the previous animals lacked. The white dog

The Bull Terrier made his first appearance in the United States in the early 1900s.

immediately became the color of choice, and the colored dog fell from favor.

However, some breeders felt that Hink's dog lacked the courage and fighting abilities of the old dogs and he was challenged to prove that his streamlined, white dog was as ferocious as the previous animals seen in the pits. Cassell's *Book of the Dog* noted "to prove his strain had lost none of its cherished quality of belligerence, Hinks matched his 40-pound bitch, Puss, against one of the old Bulldog types (60 pounds) for a five-pound note and a case of champagne. In a half hour, Puss had killed her opponent and her own injuries were so slight that she was able to appear the next morning at a dog show and take a prize for her good looks and condition."

As the breed continued to develop, less emphasis was placed upon the ability and desire to fight, and more emphasis was placed upon disposition. However, he remained an unusually strong, fast, thoroughly game dog, able to think for himself, and though injured, would never turn on his master.

By the 1870s and 1880s, White Bull Terriers were being imported into the United States and they attracted a loyal following. They were recognized by the American Kennel Club in 1891 and the Bull Terrier Club of America was founded in 1897.

In 1895, ear cropping was outlawed in England and the Bull Terrier breeder faced a further challenge—breeding for an erect ear rather than cropping the ear to achieve the smart, clean look. Within five or six years, dedicated breeders in England were able to breed for the erect ear. By 1930, it was stated in the standard that anything other than an erect ear was a fault. In America, where ear cropping has never been outlawed, breeders were still cropping ears until the late 1930s.

The Colored Bull Terrier came about through the efforts of Edward Lyon, who was hoping to produce a Miniature Bull Terrier by crossing the White Bull Terrier to the Staffordshire Terrier. He liked the colorful dog that emerged and continued to experiment with his breeding program. The breed developed slowly as breeders had to continually breed back to the Staffordshire for the color. Eventually, sufficient numbers of quality Colored Bull Terriers were produced and interbreeding was possible. Since it was no longer necessary to return to the Staffordshire, the breeders were now able to concentrate on scientific color breeding.

The standard is the same for both the White and Colored Bull Terrier, except for color. The White Bull Terrier can have color markings anywhere on the head, but any color elsewhere is severely penalized. Common head markings are eye patches and markings on the ears. The standard for the Colored variety

The spirited Bull Terrier's good temperament should be apparent in his lively expression.

Considered a separate breed, the Miniature Bull Terrier, shown here, is a smaller version of the Bull Terrier.

reads: "Any color other than white, or any color with white markings. Other things being equal, the preferred color is brindle. A dog which is predominately white shall be disqualified." Colored Bull Terriers usually have white markings on the legs, chest, neck, and head. The color must be predominant over the white. If he has few or no white markings, he is referred to as "solid."

Size separates the Miniature Bull Terrier from the standard Bull Terrier. From the 1860s, separate categories were established at shows for the two sizes. The Miniature nearly faced extinction in the early 1900s, and by 1918, the English Kennel Club

closed registrations because so few applications had been made. In 1939, a Colonial Glyn founded a club for the Miniature and new interest in the breed emerged.

The Miniature Bull Terrier resembles the standard except for his size, with shoulder height being between 10 and 14 inches. The weight of the dog is in proportion to his height. In 1945, the English Kennel Club listed the Miniature as a separate variety. In 1997, when the Bull Terrier Club of America held their centenary celebration, the Miniature Bull Terrier Club of America held its regional specialty in the next ring, this being the first time the two breeds held combined specialties.

CHARACTERISTICS OF THE BULL TERRIER

The Bull Terrier has been described in many ways: a charming and staunch friend; a true sportsman and courageous defender; a gentleman with a sweet disposition. He has endurance, gentleness, loyalty, and he is mentally sound, happy, and outgoing. He is an extrovert and a jaunty clown with a sweet disposition. Do remember, though, that this is a big, strong dog that does not take a back seat. Fear is unknown to him, and he has lost none of his courage and quick instincts.

The famous Bull Terrier breeder, E. S. Montgomery, wrote in his book, *The Bull Terrier*: "It has often been said that once a man or woman owns a Bull Terrier, he has no use for any other breed of dog. To the true Bull Terrier lover, other breeds may come and go, but Bull Terriers go on forever. There is something impossible to describe about them that no other breed possesses. They are the best of pals, never yap, are devoted to their owners and are the best tempered dogs alive, but at the

There are so many activities that you and your dog can participate in, and the versatile Bull Terrier has the ability to excel at them all! Tessi, owned by Dorinda Desmet, sails over an agility bar jump.

same time, they can, if necessary, fight as no other dog can and will allow no one to molest their owners on any pretext whatever."

Common characteristics of all terriers are their desire to work with great enthusiasm and their courage. They all have large and powerful teeth for the size of their bodies; they have keen hearing and excellent eyesight. No matter for how many generations they have been pets, the purpose for which the breed was developed will remain within the dog.

Many people thrive on the devoted companion–ship a Bull Terrier can provide.

Although some traits are inherited within a breed, every Bull Terrier is an individual with his own personality—these three friends agree!

The Bull Terrier's attachment to children is legendary, and they enjoy "clowning around" with their friends.

Probably the most distinguishing characteristic of the Bull Terrier is his egg-shaped head, which is unlike any other breed. In addition, his eyes are small and triangular, set obliquely with a "piercing glint." Add the body of the gladiator and jaunty movement and you have a unique-looking dog.

The Bull Terrier craves attention and can be persistent in his efforts to receive it. He loves to snuggle, be it next to you on the sofa or with you in bed. They are excellent with children, becoming happy companions to them. They love to play and are often called the clowns of the dog world.

He does require an owner with a firm hand because of his intelligence and fighting background. This does not mean that the owner must use harsh treatment, but it is important that the dog knows where he stands in the family hierarchy. Determine early on who is going to be the boss of the household. Use logical and firm, yet affectionate, training methods, and you and your Bull Terrier should get along well.

The Bull Terrier requires more affection than many other breeds, so this is not the breed for you if everyone in the household is gone for long hours. Take him for a walk each day, give him a cozy bed and lots of hugs, and your pet will be a happy one.

Today's Bull Terriers come in a vast array of colors, including brindle, black and white, and tri-color.

STANDARD FOR THE BULL TERRIER

The overall appearance of the Bull Terrier should be one of strength, balance, and intelligence.

WHITE

The Bull Terrier must be strongly built, muscular, symmetrical and active, with a keen determined and intelligent expression, full of fire but of sweet disposition and amenable to discipline.

Head—should be long, strong and deep right to the end of the muzzle, but not coarse. Full face it should be oval in outline and be filled completely up giving the impression of fullness with a surface devoid of hollows or indentations, i.e., egg shaped. In profile it should curve gently downwards from the top of the skull to the tip of the nose. The forehead should be flat across from ear to ear. The distance from the tip of the nose to the eyes should be perceptibly greater than that from the eyes to the top of the skull. The underjaw should be deep and well defined.

Lips—should be clean and tight.

Teeth—should meet in either a level or in a scissors bite. In the scissors bite the upper teeth should fit in front of and closely against the lower teeth, and they should be sound, strong and perfectly regular.

Ears—should be small, thin and placed close together. They should be capable of being held stiffly erect, when they should point upwards.

tapering from the shoulders to the head and it should be free from loose skin.

Chest—should be broad when viewed from in front, and there should be great depth from withers to brisket, so that the latter is nearer the ground than the belly.

Body—should be well rounded with marked spring of rib, the back should be short and strong.

Well-bred Bull Terrier puppies should exhibit characteristics of the standard almost from birth.

Eyes—should be well sunken and as dark as possible, with a piercing glint and they should be small, triangular and obliquely placed; set near together and high up on the dog's head. Blue eyes are a disqualification.

Nose—should be black, with well-developed nostrils bent downward at the tip.

Neck—should be very muscular, long, arched and clean,

The back ribs deep. Slightly arched over the loin. The shoulders should be strong and muscular but without heaviness. The shoulder blades should be wide and flat and there should be a very pronounced backward slope from the bottom edge of the blade to the top edge. Behind the shoulders there should be no slackness or dip at the withers. The underline from the brisket to

Mc.Williams Never Offside owned by William de Veer is only eight weeks old, but he already demonstrates the deliberate stance and powerful build of the Bull Terrier.

The Bull Terrier's body should possess a short back and well-knit strength with graceful lines.

the belly should form a graceful upward curve.

Legs—should be big boned but not to the point of coarseness; the forelegs should be of moderate length, perfectly straight, and the dog must stand firmly upon them. The elbows must turn neither in nor out, and the pasterns should be strong and upright. The hind legs should be parallel viewed from behind. The thighs very muscular with hocks well let down. Hind pasterns short and upright. The stifle joint should be well bent with a well-developed second thigh.

Feet—round and compact with well-arched toes like a cat.

Tail—should be short, set on low, fine, and ideally should be carried horizontally. It should be thick where it joins the body, and should taper to a fine point.

Coat—should be short, flat, harsh to the touch and with a fine gloss. The dog's skin should fit tightly.

Color—is white though markings on the head are permissible. Any markings elsewhere on the coat are to be severely faulted. Skin pigmentation is not to be penalized.

Movement—The dog shall move smoothly, covering the ground with free, easy strides, fore and hind legs should move parallel each to each when viewed from in front or behind. The forelegs reaching out well and the hind legs moving smoothly at the hip and flexing well at the stifle and hock. The dog should move compactly and in one piece but with a typical jaunty air that suggests agility and power.

The head of the Bull Terrier should be clean cut, long, and deep, with a vivacious and animated expression.

Faults

Any departure from the foregoing points shall be considered a fault and the seriousness of the fault shall be in exact proportion to its degree, i.e.,

It must be remembered that the Bull Terrier is first and foremost an active and energetic dog, and this should always be reflected in his conformation and temperament.

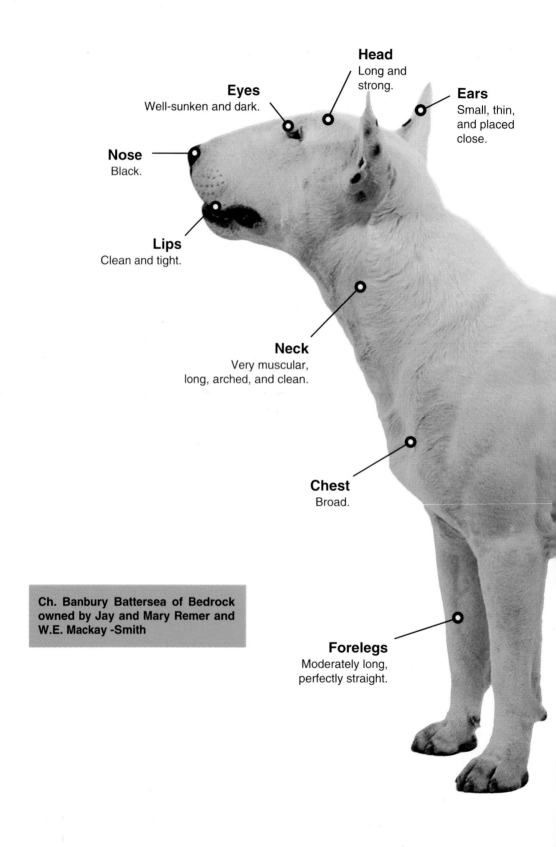

Head
Long and strong.

Eyes
Well-sunken and dark.

Ears
Small, thin, and placed close.

Nose
Black.

Lips
Clean and tight.

Neck
Very muscular, long, arched, and clean.

Chest
Broad.

Ch. Banbury Battersea of Bedrock owned by Jay and Mary Remer and W.E. Mackay -Smith

Forelegs
Moderately long, perfectly straight.

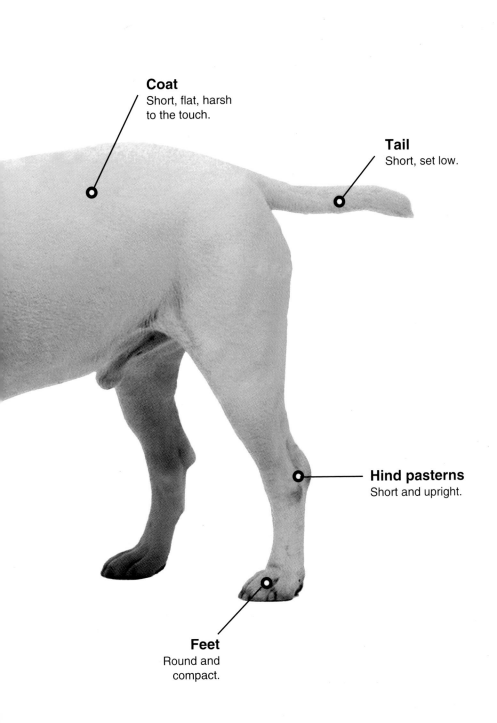

Coat
Short, flat, harsh to the touch.

Tail
Short, set low.

Hind pasterns
Short and upright.

Feet
Round and compact.

The Bull Terrier's coat should be short, flat, and harsh to the touch and always appear healthy and shiny.

a very crooked front is a very bad fault; a rather crooked front is a rather bad fault; and a slightly crooked front is a slight fault.

DISQUALIFICATION
Blue eyes.
COLORED
The Standard for the Colored Variety is the same as for the White except for the sub head "Color" which reads: *Color.* Any color other than white, or any color with white markings. Other things being equal, the preferred color is brindle. A dog that is predominantly white shall be disqualified.

DISQUALIFICATIONS
Blue eyes.
Any dog which is predominantly white.
Approved July 9, 1974

SELECTING YOUR BULL TERRIER

When purchasing a Bull Terrier, be sure to buy your dog from a reputable breeder. Ask to see the dam (and the sire, if on the premises) and inquire as to

Because of the relative rarity of the breed, be prepared to wait for your puppy once you have determined that this is the breed for you. You may have to wait six

Be sure to do your homework and learn all you can about the breed before making the decision to bring a Bull Terrier puppy into your home.

whether the breeder belongs to the local all-breed kennel club or the Bull Terrier Club of America.

The White Bull Terrier was around 75th in popularity on a recent list of American Kennel Club breeds, and the Miniature Bull Terrier was down around 120. This is not a breed like the German Shepherd Dog, for which you will find ten ads for puppies in the Sunday paper.

or eight months and you may have to travel to find the right dog. Take your time. When you buy a car, you may keep it three years and then trade it in for a new model. When buying a puppy, you are making a commitment that can last anywhere from 10 to 15 years. Be sure you know what you are buying and be sure to get what you want!

If there is a regional Bull Terrier club in your town or state, do make contact and ask for assistance in finding a puppy. Members of the Bull Terrier club are there to help new–comers to the breed. They want to make certain

Your Bull Terrier will have a good start in life if his parents are happy and well-adjusted. Try to see the dam and sire of the puppy you are considering.

that this is the breed for you and that you will make a good Bull Terrier owner. On occasion, there may be an older dog that for one reason or another needs a home. Do give this consideration, as an older dog can be a joy to bring into the household as well.

The standard of the breed will give you an idea of what you are looking for in a Bull Terrier. E. S. Montgomery summed it up very neatly: "Of all the terriers, as attractive as they may be, the Bull Terrier is the most symmetrical in appearance and most elegant of outline; he is the most distinctive of all dogs; he is particularly handsome and he is most beautifully proportioned with a build that embodies elegance of form and fiber that suggests agility, strength, and activity. His graceful but sturdy lines, his long but well-filled-up head, and the remarkable beauty of his symmetry, make him unusually striking and pleasing to the eye. The short coat makes him desirable for the house for there he is man's best companion."

Choosing a male or female dog is a matter of preference, either sex will make a wonderful companion.

YOUR HEALTHY BULL TERRIER

William Haynes wrote in 1925, "The terrier owner is a 'lucky Devil' for his dogs do not, as a rule, spend a great deal of time in the hospital. All members of the terrier family, from the giant of the race, the Airedale, way down to little Scottie, owe a big debt to Nature for having blessed them with remarkably robust constitutions. Even when really sick, they make wonderfully rapid recoveries. It is almost a joke to keep such a naturally healthy dog as a terrier in the pink of condition. All he needs is dry, clean kennels with decent bedding; good, nourishing food at regular hours; all the fresh water

Your Bull Terrier puppy will look to you, his owner, to provide for all his needs.

Through breeding dogs of only the best quality, we are assured that good health and temperament will be passed down to each new generation.

Your energetic Bull Terrier puppy will need plenty of exercise and playtime outdoors to stay healthy.

A thorough examination of your Bull Terrier's mouth, teeth, and gums should be part of his annual checkup.

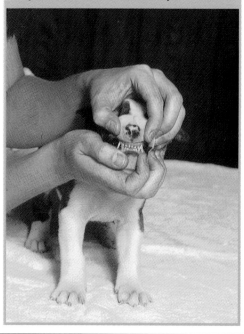

he wants to drink; plenty of exercise; and a little grooming. Given these few things a terrier will be disgustingly well, full of high spirits, and happy as a clam at high tide."

A Bull Terrier is a thrifty dog. Give him care, use your common sense, and have a good veterinarian available. Find a reliable veterinarian that you trust, take your dog in when you think that he has a problem, follow any instructions given to you, and if there is a problem, recovery will usually be very rapid. The average life span of a Bull Terrier is ten years, slightly shorter than that of other terriers, many of which have a tendency to live very long lives in the canine world.

A healthy Bull Terrier puppy will look forward to mealtime and have a voracious appetite.

Regular medical care is extremely important throughout your Bull Terrier's life. Vaccination boosters and physical exams are part of your dog's lifelong maintenance.

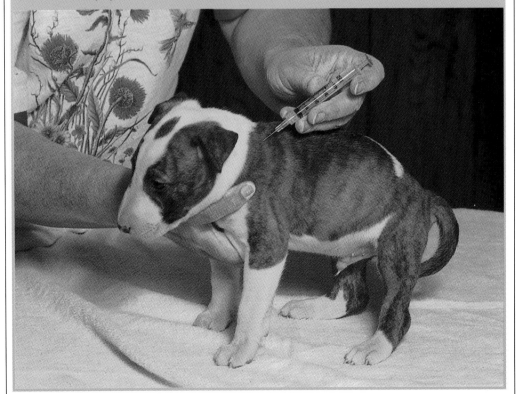

Your dog should have yearly inoculations, along with having a stool sample tested to make certain that he is free from worms. Keep his teeth clean and his nails trimmed. Your veterinarian can do these jobs if you or your groomer are unable to do so. Watch for ticks in the summer. Any wounds should be cleaned out; some of them may require veterinary care. Yearly heartworm checks in some areas of the country are also important.

If your veterinarian is not available at odd hours for emergencies, know where the emergency veterinarian is located and keep his telephone number handy. Many veterinarians in large cities no longer have an emergency service and you must rely on these special facilities for late evening, weekend, and holiday services. Keep your dog groomed and clean. Limit his exposure to the sun in the summer, and certainly *never* leave him in the car on a hot day.

Your dog should be kept either in a fenced yard or on a leash. It's foolish and often against the law to let your dog run loose and take a chance of being run over by a car. Too often, the story is heard about the dog that lives at the end of the cul-de-sac where only one delivery truck comes a day, and that truck runs the dog over. It only takes one vehicle to shorten a dog's life.

Several problems in the Bull Terrier that you should be aware of are deafness and atopy, or skin

Be sure to provide your puppy with plenty of safe toys to play with, the Nylabone®️ Frisbee™️ is just the thing! *The trademark Frisbee is used under license from Mattel, Inc., California, USA.

You'll surely fall in love with your Bull Terrier puppy. It is important to be aware of any particular health problems concerning the breed.

allergy. The first priority in avoiding the purchase of a puppy with a hereditary fault is to acquire your dog from a reputable breeder, as was previously mentioned.

Deafness, thought to be a factor in breeding white dogs only to white dogs, as had been done early in the breed's history, is not nearly as serious a problem now as it was at one time. Deafness can be a problem in any of the white-coated breeds. Breeders now have their puppies tested and this can be done on puppies as early as eight weeks to determine if there is a hearing problem.

Skin allergies are more prevalent in the white dogs. If you find your dog to be persistently chewing or licking on a particular part of his body, such as his feet, he should be taken to a veterinarian who has some knowledge of skin diseases and allergies. Sometimes the itching can be controlled by an over-the-counter medication.

Cancer can be diagnosed in any breed of dog, and Bull Terriers are no exception. As in man, there is not always a cure and early detection is the best form of prevention. Check your dog over each time you groom him for any lumps or bumps that you have not noticed before. Fast-growing lumps are cause for concern, particularly when found around

As your Bull Terrier grows older, his needs will gradually change, you may need to adjust his routine to keep him happy and well.

the mammary glands in females. Have a veterinarian check any lump that you are concerned about.

THE GERIATRIC DOG

The geriatric dog—a dog over eight years of age—may require a little more care, or different care, than the younger dog. As your dog ages, he will slow down and possibly develop some arthritis. His sight and hearing may start to wane and he may sleep more. Let him have his way. Do not expect him to take the three-mile walk he enjoyed as a pup. You may want to try special dog food formulated for the geriatric or sedate dog. Be sure that he has a warm place to sleep and try to keep him at a normal weight, as excess weight can be difficult on the rheumatoid bones.

As he ages and becomes more infirm, you will eventually be confronted with the decision of putting your dog down. Unfortunately, dogs and humans do not die very often in their sleep. With the dog, though, we are able to make the decision to be a humane owner, and the day may come when you must take your pet in to be euthanized by your veterinarian. It is hard to know when it is time, but again, use your common sense and try not to let the dog suffer unduly.

YOUR NEW BULL TERRIER PUPPY

SELECTION

When you do pick out a Bull Terrier puppy as a pet, don't be hasty; the longer you study puppies, the better you will understand them. Make it your transcendent concern to select only one that radiates good health plays coy behind other puppies or people, or hides his head under your arm or jacket appealing to your protective instinct. Pick the Bull Terrier puppy who forthrightly picks you! The feeling of attraction should be mutual!

Upon selection of your Bull Terrier puppy, the breeder should offer a guarantee against inherited disorders.

and spirit and is lively on his feet, whose eyes are bright, whose coat shines, and who comes forward eagerly to make and to cultivate your acquaintance. Don't fall for any shy little darling that wants to retreat to his bed or his box, or

DOCUMENTS

Now, a little paper work is in order. When you purchase a purebred Bull Terrier puppy, you should receive a transfer of ownership, registration material, and other "papers" (a list of the

In early life your Bull Terrier will receive most of his nourishment from his mother. Once he arrives at your home, be sure his diet includes all the nutrients he needs.

immunization shots, if any, the puppy may have been given; a note on whether or not the puppy has been wormed; a diet and feeding schedule to which the puppy is accustomed) and you are welcomed as a fellow owner to a long, pleasant association with a most lovable pet, and more (news)paper work.

GENERAL PREPARATION

You have chosen to own a particular Bull Terrier puppy. You have chosen it very carefully over all other breeds and all other puppies. So before you ever get that Bull Terrier puppy home, you will have prepared for its arrival

They may be tiny now, but Bull Terrier puppies attain most of their adult size by six months of age.

Dogs are a very important part of their owners' lives and the bond between humans and animals is a strong one.

Encourage your puppy to explore the world around him. New experiences will enrich his life and make him an active participant in his own socialization.

by reading everything you can get your hands on having to do with the management of Bull Terriers and puppies. True, you will run into many conflicting opinions, but at least you will not be starting "blind." Read, study, digest. Talk over your plans with your veterinarian, other "Bull Terrier people," and the seller of your Bull Terrier puppy.

All puppies need to chew, and Bull Terrier puppies are no different. Provide safe and healthy Nylabone® toys for your puppies' enjoyment.

When you get your Bull Terrier puppy, you will find that your reading and study are far from finished. You've just scratched the surface in your plan to provide the greatest possible comfort and health for your Bull Terrier, by the same token, you do want to assure yourself of the greatest possible enjoyment of this

minutes. Have newspapers handy in case of car-sickness. If you are driving alone a covered carton lined with newspapers provides protection for puppy and car. Avoid excitement and unnecessary handling of the puppy on arrival. A Bull Terrier puppy is a very small "package" to be making a complete change of

A puppy is a particularly social creature and needs the company of other puppies when young. The more people and animals he meets, the better socialized he will become.

wonderful creature. You must be ready for this puppy mentally as well as in the physical requirements.

TRANSPORTATION

If you take the puppy home by car, protect him from drafts, particularly in cold weather. Wrapped in a towel and carried in the arms or lap of a passenger, the Bull Terrier puppy will usually make the trip without mishap. If the pup starts to drool and to squirm, stop the car for a few

surroundings and company, and he needs frequent rest and refreshment to renew his vitality.

THE FIRST DAY AND NIGHT

When your Bull Terrier puppy arrives in your home, put him down on the floor and don't pick him up again, except when it is absolutely necessary. He is a dog, a real dog, and must not be lugged around like a rag doll. Handle him as little as possible, and permit no one to pick him up and baby him. To repeat, *put your*

Bull Terrier puppy on the floor or the ground and let him stay there except when it may be necessary to do otherwise.

Quite possibly your Bull Terrier puppy will be afraid for a while in his new surroundings, without his mother and littermates. Comfort him and reassure him, but don't console him. Don't give him the "oh-you-poor-itsy-bitsy-puppy" treatment. Be calm, friendly, and reassuring. Encourage him to walk around and sniff over his new home. If it's dark, put on the lights. Let him roam for a few minutes while you and everyone else concerned sit quietly or go about your routine business. Let the puppy come back to you.

Playmates may cause an immediate problem if the new Bull Terrier puppy is to be greeted by children or other pets. If not, you can skip this subject. The natural affinity between puppies and children calls for some supervision until a live-and-let-live relationship is established. This applies particularly to a Christmas puppy, when there is more excitement than usual and

more chance for a puppy to swallow something upsetting. It is a better plan to welcome the puppy several days before or after the holiday week. Like a baby, your Bull Terrier puppy needs much rest and should not be overhandled. Once a child realizes that a puppy has "feelings" similar to his own, and can readily be hurt or injured, the opportunities for play and responsibilities provide exercise and training for both.

It is important to remember that when your Bull Terrier puppy is young he will need you to reassure and guide him through his first few days at your home.

For his first night with you, he should be put where he is to sleep every night—say in the kitchen, since its floor can usually be easily cleaned. Let him explore the kitchen to his heart's content; close doors to confine him there. Prepare his food and feed him lightly the first night. Give him a pan with some water in it—not a lot, since most puppies will try to drink the whole pan dry. Give him an old coat or shirt to lie on. Since a coat or shirt will be strong in human scent, he will pick it out to lie on, thus furthering his feeling of security in the room where he has just been fed.

Your puppy will need proper socialization from the very beginning if he is to become a valued member of your household.

HOUSEBREAKING HELPS

Now, sooner or later—mostly sooner—your new Bull Terrier puppy is going to "puddle" on the floor. First take a newspaper and lay it on the puddle until the urine is soaked up onto the paper. *Save this paper.* Now take a cloth with soap and water, wipe up the floor and dry it well. Then take the wet paper and place it on a fairly large square of newspapers in a convenient corner. When cleaning up, always keep a piece of wet paper on top of the others. Every time he wants to "squat," he will seek out this spot and use the papers. (This routine is rarely necessary for more than three days.) Now leave your Bull Terrier puppy for the night. Quite probably he will cry and howl a bit; some are more stubborn than others on this matter. But let him stay alone for the night. This may seem like harsh treatment, but it is the best procedure in the long run. Just let him cry; he will weary of it sooner or later.

Puppies can fall into all sorts of predicaments—be sure to confine them in a safe place when they are not closely supervised.

FEEDING YOUR BULL TERRIER

Now let's talk about feeding your Bull Terrier, a subject so simple that it's amazing there is so much nonsense and misunderstanding about it. Is it expensive to feed a Bull Terrier?

with great variety (and possibly turn them into poor, "picky" eaters) they will eat almost anything that they become accustomed to. Many dogs flatly refuse to eat nice, fresh beef. They

Consult your breeder or veterinarian about the appropriate diet for your Bull Terrier.

No, it is not! You can feed your Bull Terrier economically and keep him in perfect shape the year round, or you can feed him expensively. He'll thrive either way, and let's see why this is true.

First of all, remember a Bull Terrier is a dog. Dogs do not have a high degree of selectivity in their food, and unless you spoil them

pick around it and eat everything else. But meat—bah! Why? They aren't accustomed to it! They'd eat rabbit fast enough, but they refuse beef because they aren't used to it.

VARIETY NOT NECESSARY

A good general rule of thumb is forget all human preferences and

POPpups™ are healthy treats for your Bull Terrier. When bone-hard they help to control plaque build-up; when microwaved they become a rich cracker, which your Bull Terrier will love. The POPpup™ is available in liver and other flavors and is fortified with calcium.

A healthy and tasty treat for your Bull Terrier because they love cheese is Chooz™. Chooz™ are bone-hard but can be micro–waved to expand into a huge, crispy dog biscuit. They are almost fat free and about 70 percent protein.

don't give a thought to variety. Choose the right diet for your Bull Terrier and feed it to him day after day, year after year, winter and summer. But what is the right diet?

Hundreds of thousands of dollars have been spent in canine nutrition research. The results are pretty conclusive, so you needn't go into a lot of experimenting with trials of this and that every other week. Research has proven just what your dog needs to eat and to keep healthy.

DOG FOOD

There are almost as many right diets as there are dog experts, but the basic diet most often

These Bull Terrier puppies are growing in leaps and bounds and will need especially nutritious meals to help them develop into healthy adults.

recommended is one that consists of a dry food, either meal or kibble form. There are several of excellent quality, manufactured by reliable companies, research tested, and nationally advertised. They are inexpensive, highly satisfactory, and easily available in stores everywhere in containers of five to 50 pounds. Larger amounts cost less per pound, usually.

If you have a choice of brands, it is usually safer to choose the better known one but even so, carefully read the analysis on the package. Do not choose any food in which the protein level is less than 25 percent, and be sure that this protein comes from both animal and vegetable sources. The good dog foods have meat meal, fish meal, liver, and such, plus protein from alfalfa and soy beans, as well as some dried milk product. Note the vitamin content carefully. See that they are there in good proportions and be especially certain that the food contains the proper high levels of vitamins A and D, two of the most perishable and important ones. Note the B-complex level, but don't worry about carbohydrate and mineral levels. These substances are plentiful and cheap and not likely to be lacking in a good brand.

The advice given for how to choose a dry food also applies to moist or canned types of dog foods, if you decide to use one of these.

This Bull Terrier seems to be enjoying a romp in the outdoors. Remember that proper nutrition will help to keep your dog in good health.

Looks like this Bull Terrier has decided to help himself to a snack!

Be sure to provide your Bull Terrier puppy with cool, clean water at all times.

Having chosen a really good food, feed it to your Bull Terrier as the manufacturer directs. And once you've started, stick to it. Never change if you can possibly help it. A switch from one meal or kibble-type food can usually be made without too much upset; however, a change will almost invariably give you (and your Bull Terrier) some trouble.

WHEN SUPPLEMENTS ARE NEEDED

Now what about supplements of various kinds, mineral and vitamin, or the various oils? They are all okay to add to your Bull Terrier's food. However, if you are feeding your Bull Terrier a correct diet, and this is easy to do, no supplements are necessary unless your Bull Terrier has been improperly fed, has been sick, or is having puppies. Vitamins and minerals are naturally present in all the foods; and to ensure against any loss through processing, they are added in concentrated form to the dog food you use. Except on the advice of your veterinarian, added amounts of vitamins can prove harmful to your Bull Terrier! The same risk goes with minerals.

FEEDING SCHEDULE

When and how much food to give your Bull Terrier? Most dogs do better if fed two or three smaller meals per day—this is not only better but vital to larger and deep-chested dogs. As to how to prepare the food and how much to give, it is generally best to follow the directions on the food package. Your own Bull Terrier may want a little more or a little less.

Fresh, cool water should always be available to your Bull Terrier. This is important to good health throughout his lifetime.

ALL BULL TERRIERS NEED TO CHEW

Puppies and young Bull Terriers need something with resistance to chew on while their teeth and jaws are developing—for cutting the puppy teeth; to induce growth of the permanent teeth under the puppy teeth; to assist in getting rid of the puppy teeth at the proper time; to help the permanent teeth through the gums; to ensure normal jaw development; and to settle the permanent teeth solidly in the jaws.

The adult Bull Terrier's desire to chew stems from the instinct for tooth cleaning, gum massage, and jaw exercise—plus the need for an outlet for periodic doggie tensions.

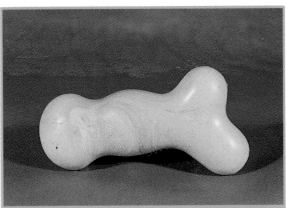

The Galileo™ is the toughest nylon bone ever made. It is flavored to appeal to your Bull Terrier and has a relatively soft outer layer. It is a necessary chew toy and doggy pacifier.

This is why dogs, especially puppies and young dogs, will often destroy property worth hundreds of dollars when their chewing instinct is not diverted from their owner's possessions. And this is why you should provide your Bull Terrier with something to chew—something that has the necessary functional qualities, is desirable from the Bull Terrier's viewpoint, and is safe for him.

It is very important that your Bull Terrier not be permitted to chew on anything he can break or on any indigestible thing from which he can bite sizable chunks. Sharp pieces, such as from a bone which can be broken by a dog, may pierce the intestinal wall and kill. Indigestible things that can be bitten off in chunks, such as from shoes or rubber or plastic toys, may cause an intestinal stoppage (if not regurgitated) and bring on a painful death, unless surgery is promptly performed.

Strong natural bones, such as 4- to 8-inch lengths of round shin bone from mature beef—either the kind you can get from a butcher or one of the varieties available commercially in pet stores—may serve your Bull Terrier's teething needs if his mouth is large enough to handle them effectively. You may be tempted to give your Bull Terrier puppy a smaller bone and he may not be able to break it when you do, but puppies grow rapidly and the power of their jaws constantly increases until maturity. This means that a growing Bull Terrier may break one of the smaller bones at any time, swallow the pieces, and die painfully before you realize what is wrong.

All hard natural bones are very abrasive. If your Bull Terrier is an avid chewer, natural bones may wear away his teeth prematurely; hence, they then should be taken away from your dog when the teething purposes have been served. The badly worn, and usually painful, teeth of many mature dogs can be traced to excessive chewing on natural bones.

Contrary to popular belief, knuckle bones that can be chewed up and swallowed by your Bull Terrier provide little, if any, usable calcium or other nutriment. They do, however, disturb the digestion of most dogs and cause them to vomit the nourishing food they need.

Dried rawhide products of various types, shapes, sizes, and prices are available on the market and have become quite popular. However, they don't serve the primary chewing functions very well; they are a bit messy when wet from mouthing, and most Bull Terriers chew them up rather rapidly—but they have been considered safe for dogs until recently. Now, more and more incidents of death, and near death, by strangulation have been reported to be the results of partially swallowed chunks of rawhide swelling in the throat. More recently, some veterinarians have been attributing cases of acute constipation to large pieces of incompletely digested rawhide in the intestine.

A new product, molded rawhide, is very safe. During the

Your puppy deserves the best! Provide him with plenty of safe and healthy chew toys while he is teething, like this Nylabone® Frisbee™.

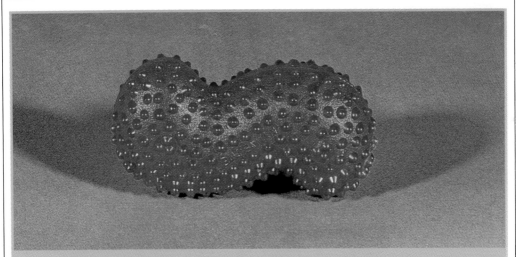

The Hercules™ is made of very tough polyurethane. It is designed for Bull Terriers who are extremely strong chewers. The raised dental tips massage the gums and mechanically remove the plaque they encounter during chewing.

process, the rawhide is melted and then injection molded into the familiar dog shape. It is very hard and is eagerly accepted by Bull Terriers. The melting process also sterilizes the rawhide. Don't confuse this with pressed rawhide, which is nothing more than small strips of rawhide squeezed together.

The nylon bones, especially those with natural meat and bone fractions added, are probably the most complete, safe, and economical answer to the chewing need. Dogs cannot break them or

All Bull Terriers require some vegetable matter in their diet. The Carrot Bone™ made by Nylabone® helps to control plaque and is a healthy treat for your Bull Terrier.

bite off sizable chunks; hence, they are completely safe—and being longer lasting than other things offered for the purpose, they are economical.

Hard chewing raises little bristle-like projections on the surface of the nylon bones—to provide effective interim tooth cleaning and vigorous gum massage, much in the same way your toothbrush does it for you. The little projections are raked off and swallowed in the form of thin shavings, but the chemistry of the nylon is such that they break down in the stomach fluids and pass through without effect.

The toughness of the nylon provides the strong chewing resistance needed for important jaw exercise and effectively aids teething functions, but there is no tooth wear because nylon is non-abrasive. Being inert, nylon does not support the growth of micro–organisms; and it can be washed in soap and water or it can be sterilized by boiling or in an autoclave.

Nylabone® is highly recommended by veterinarians as a safe, healthy nylon bone that can't splinter or chip. Nylabone® is frizzled by the dog's chewing action, creating a toothbrush-like surface that cleanses the teeth and massages the gums. Nylabone® is superior to the cheaper bones because it is made of virgin nylon, which is the strongest and longest-lasting type of nylon available. The cheaper bones are made from recycled or reground nylon scraps, and have a tendency to break apart and split easily.

Nothing, however, substitutes for periodic professional attention for your Bull Terrier's teeth and gums, not any more than your toothbrush can do that for you. Have your Bull Terrier's teeth cleaned at least once a year by your veterinarian (twice a year is better) and he will be happier, healthier, and far more pleasant to live with.

If your Bull Terrier would rather chew than do anything else, the Gumabone™ is for him. Offer him a Gumabone™ made of non-toxic, durable polyurethane to sink his teeth into.

GROOMING YOUR BULL TERRIER

Understand that when you purchase a dog, you take on the responsibility of maintaining him. Think of it in terms of your child—you bathe your youngster, comb his hair, and put a clean set of clothes on him. The result is a child that smells good, looks nice, and whom you enjoy having in your company. It is the same with your dog—keep the dog brushed and clean and you will find it a pleasure to be with him. Fortunately, owners of the Bull Terrier have a minimum of grooming to do, compared to the owners of heavily groomed terriers like the Wire Fox or the Scottish Terrier.

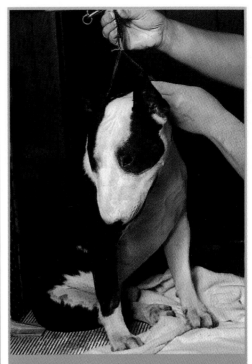

Grooming your Bull Terrier on a specially made grooming table with a harness will help to keep him safe and still during your sessions.

Never allow your Bull Terrier puppy to remain wet after a bath. Wrap him in a clean towel and dry him thoroughly.

Grooming will consist primarily of a weekly "go-over." Here are the tools that you will need:

1. A grooming table, something sturdy with a rubber mat covering the top. You will need a grooming arm or a hanger. You can use a table in your laundry room with an eyehook in the ceiling for holding the leash. Your dog will be comfortable even if confined, and thus you will be able to work on the dog. Grooming—especially when trimming the toenails—can be a frustrating job if you attempt it without a table and a grooming arm.

You must never ignore your Bull Terrier's feet during grooming. Check for cracked footpads and keep his nails trimmed short to prevent injury.

canal. Always check for any unusual lumps or bumps when grooming your dog.

If he needs a bath, put him in a tub and give him a good bathing and rinsing. Be sure to rinse all the shampoo out of his coat, as any residue could cause skin irritation. After toweling him down, return him to the grooming table. This is a good time to trim his toenails, as they will be soft and easier to trim. You will also find that a bath will loosen any dead coat. After the bath is complete, be sure to brush him out thoroughly, as this will clean out dead undercoat hairs.

You may want to trim the facial whiskers to the skin, as this will give the dog a neat, clean-cut look. Wipe him dry with a towel or

2. A bristle brush, a grooming glove, and a toenail trimmer.

3. Cotton balls and swabs and old washcloths.

To start: Set your dog on the table and put the leash around his neck. Have your leash up behind the ears and keep it taut when you fasten it to your eyehook or to the hanger. Do not walk away and leave your dog unattended as he may jump off the table and injure himself.

Brush him out and wipe him down with a damp washcloth. Check his eyes for redness or irritation and clean them with a damp cotton ball. Check the ears. Take a swab dipped in alcohol and gently clean them, being careful not to go into the ear

Brushing your dog's teeth is recom‐mended by every veterinarian. Use the 2-Brush™ regularly, 3-4 times per week and you may never need your veterinarian to do the job for you.

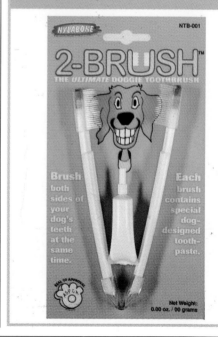

This lovely Bull Terrier obviously enjoys showing off her good grooming for the camera!

If you accustom your Bull Terrier to regular grooming, he will come to think of it as an enjoyable experience.

use a hair dryer on a cool setting. If it is a nice, sunny day, you may want to put him outside to dry.

If you are showing your Bull Terrier, you can rub him down with pomade to give his coat a high gloss. In addition, a twice-weekly brushing, along with a healthy diet, will also keep the coat shiny. Trimming for show will be minimal, and the purpose will be to neaten up the dog's appearance. Pluck any of the few out-of-place hairs with your fingers to give a neat look. If showing, be sure to trim the facial whiskers.

Voila! You are finished! Smooth-coated dogs are low maintenance and those of us who own one appreciate it!

Of course, if you want to take the easy way out, you can eliminate all of the grooming for yourself and take your dog to the groomer every couple of months to have him bathed and have his toenails trimmed. However, when you have a breed that is as easy to groom as the Bull Terrier, it seems a shame to leave the job up to someone else! Besides, the time you spend on grooming with your dog will result in a closer bond between dog and owner.

Again, your pet should be brushed weekly and bathed as needed. The toenails should be trimmed every month or so. Follow this easy plan and your dog will smell good, be clean, and it will be a pleasure to be in his company!

SHOWING YOUR BULL TERRIER

The prestigious Westminster Kennel Club dog show, held every year in the beginning of February in New York City, is the second oldest annual sporting event in the United States, with only the Kentucky Derby having greater longevity.

If you are new to the show ring, you should attend a few local have a good dog, this may be the sport and hobby for you.

Contact your local all-breed club and find out if they offer conformation classes in which you can learn how to handle your dog in the ring. Start attending these classes on a regular basis. One class does not an expert make! The all-breed club will hold

It is important to remember that your Bull Terrier wants to please you and with patience will learn what you have to teach him!

shows without your dog to see what the game is about. If you are competitive, have the time and money to compete and, of course, one or two matches a year and you should plan to attend them. Match shows are run like a dog show, but they are casual and a good place for the beginner to learn. You will not receive any points toward a championship, but you will find out how a dog show is run, and you will learn what will be expected of you and your dog. Entry fees are minimal. This is also a good opportunity to meet the people involved in the breed.

When you think you are ready—when your dog can walk on a lead and you feel a tiny bit of confidence—enter an AKC-licensed dog show.

Remember that participating successfully in dog shows requires patience, time, money, skill, and talent. It is one of the few sporting competitions in which amateurs and professionals compete on equal footing. The average dog show competitor remains active for only four to five years. Personal commitments such as children, work, and other hobbies can be a problem for those who want to compete every weekend. More often, the competitor who does not win enough will find his interest in the sport waning. A poorly groomed dog, a poorly bred dog, a dog that does not like to show, or a handler who will not take the time to learn how to handle well are all deterrents to a long stay in the sport of dog showing.

It is always a pleasure to see a good Bull Terrier in the ring. He is a smart, muscular dog, and a good one will show like a trooper. Ch. Haymarket Faultless was Best in Show at the Westminster Kennel Club show in 1918. In 1983, Ch. Banbury Benson of Bedrock, an

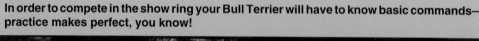

In order to compete in the show ring your Bull Terrier will have to know basic commands—practice makes perfect, you know!

owner-handled Colored Bull Terrier, was the winner of the Terrier Group at Westminster. Many Bull Terriers, White and Colored, have won Best in Show at all-breed shows throughout the country.

The Bull Terrier Club of America offers the Silverwood Competition. This is the most prestigious show for the breed because it brings out the top competition throughout the nation to compete for the best American-bred Bull Terrier. Breeders show their stock, fanciers have the opportunity to see the upcoming winners in the breed, old friendships are renewed, and new acquaintances are made. In addition, seminars and meetings covering health, conformation, and possible problems concerning the breed are held. For those who are active in breeding and showing the Bull Terrier, this is an event not to be missed.

There is only one material suitable for flossing human teeth and that's nylon. So why not get a chew toy that will enable you to interact with your Bull Terrier while it promotes dental health. As you play tug-of-war with a Nylafloss™, you'll be slowly pulling the nylon strand through your dog's teeth.

In conformation, your dog is judged by how closely he conforms to the breed standard.

TRAINING YOUR BULL TERRIER

You owe proper training to your Bull Terrier. The right and privilege of being trained are his birthright; and whether your Bull Terrier is going to be a handsome, well-mannered housedog and companion, a show dog, or whatever possible use he may be put to, the basic training is always the same—all must start with basic obedience, or what might be called "manner training."

Your Bull Terrier must come instantly when called and obey the "Sit" or "Down" command just as fast; he must walk quietly at "Heel," whether on or off lead. He must be mannerly and polite wherever he goes; he must be polite to strangers on the street and in stores. He must be mannerly in the presence of other dogs. He must not bark at children on roller skates, motorcycles, or other domestic animals. And he must be restrained from chasing cats. It is not a dog's inalienable right to chase cats, and he must be reprimanded for it.

PROFESSIONAL TRAINING

How do you go about this training? Well, it's a very simple procedure, and pretty well

Training will be much more successful if you keep it fun and interesting. Although gentle correction will sometimes be necessary, it will all prove worthwhile in the end.

standardized by now. First, if you can afford the extra expense, you may send your Bull Terrier to a professional trainer, where in 30 to 60 days he will learn how to be a "good dog." If you enlist the services of a good professional trainer, follow his advice of when to come see the dog. No, he won't forget you, but too-frequent visits at the wrong time may slow down his training progress. And using a "pro" trainer means that you will have to go for some training, too, after the trainer feels your Bull Terrier is ready to go home. You will have to learn how your Bull Terrier works, just what to expect of him and how to use what the dog has learned after he is home.

Make sure that your Bull Terrier has plenty of positive reinforcement like treats and praise during training, and in no time he'll be obeying every command.

This alert Bull Terrier eagerly awaits his owner's next command.

OBEDIENCE TRAINING CLASS

Another way to train your Bull Terrier (many experienced Bull Terrier people think this is the best) is to join an obedience training class right in your own community. There is such a group in nearly every community nowadays. Here you will be working with a group of people who are also just starting out. You will actually be training your own dog, since all work is done under the direction of a head trainer who will make suggestions to you and also tell you when and how to correct your Bull Terrier's errors. Then, too, working with such a group, your Bull Terrier will learn to get along with other

Group training classes are not only a wonderful way to teach basic obedience commands, but also offer an invaluable opportunity for socialization.

dogs. And, what is more important, he will learn to do exactly what he is told to do, no matter how much confusion there is around him or how great the temptation is to go his own way.

Write to your national kennel club for the location of a training club or class in your locality. Sign up. Go to it regularly—every session! Go early and leave late! Both you and your Bull Terrier will benefit tremendously.

TRAIN HIM BY THE BOOK

The third way of training your Bull Terrier is by the book. Yes, you can do it this way and do a good job of it too. But in using the book method, select a book, buy it, study it carefully; then study it some more, until the procedures are almost second nature to you. Then start your training. But stay with the book and its advice and exercises. Don't start in and then make up a few rules of your own. If you don't follow the book, you'll get into jams you can't get out of by yourself. If, after a few hours of short training sessions, your Bull Terrier is still not working as he should, get back to the book for a study session, because it's your fault, not the dog's! The procedures of dog training have been so well systemized that it must be your fault, since literally thousands of fine Bull Terriers have been trained by the book.

After your Bull Terrier is "letter perfect" under all conditions, then, if you wish, go on to advanced training and trick work.

Your Bull Terrier will love his obedience training, and you'll burst with pride at the finished product! Your Bull Terrier will enjoy life even more, and you'll enjoy your Bull Terrier more. And remember—you *owe good training to your Bull Terrier.*

WORKING WITH A BULL TERRIER

Every Bull Terrier should be able to lie around the house, have a good meal, receive love and attention, and be taken for a walk or a romp every day. However, some owners like the challenge of working with their dog, training him to follow commands, and seeing him perform the chores for which he was bred. With terriers, an owner can work on obedience, including tracking or utility, or train for agility. It is surely a challenge to work a terrier, but it

Your Bull Terrier can be trained to do anything—this guy looks ready for a rousing game of fetch.

can be done, and an owner can have a tremendous feeling of accomplishment once a goal is achieved.

OBEDIENCE

This is not an easy breed to work with in obedience, for even with the terriers' intelligence and independent spirit, they can sometimes be more difficult to train than had been anticipated. You will see an abundance of Golden Retrievers, Poodles, and Miniature Schnauzers in obedience classes as these breeds are easy to work with. Not only are they intelligent, but more importantly, they have a willingness to please their master.

For obedience work, dog and handler each need aptitude and determination. The handler must take time to work with the dog every day, even if it is only for five minutes or so. The handler must also have patience, and the dog must have a desire to perform and, at least, some willingness to please. Once this match is made, a handler and his dog can be well on their way toward an obedience degree, and the handler will feel a tremendous amount of achievement and accomplishment to have such a smart dog working by his side. Spectators at a dog show love to watch the action in the obedience rings, as they can understand what the dog is doing (or not doing) much better than when they watch the conformation rings.

Obedience classes are offered throughout the country, and unless you live in a very remote area, there should be a selection of training clubs from which to choose. Some classes are offered

The playful Bull Terrier needs regular activity and will enjoy a romp in the yard.

by private individuals, others by obedience or all-breed clubs. There are different methods of instruction, and you may find it worthwhile to visit various classes to see which method of training you prefer.

Many Bull Terriers have completed their obedience degrees, and even if they do not pass all of their tests, you will have a companion who minds his manners and will be easier to live with.

AGILITY

Agility is a relatively new sport that came to the United States from England. The handler and the dog, working as a team, go through a timed obstacle course. Scoring is simple, and the objective is based upon the dog completing all of the obstacles, as well as the speed with which this is accomplished.

In order to compete in this sport, you must belong to an all-breed club or an obedience club where there are individuals who support this event. The obstacle course requires substantial space and the obstacles themselves are extensive.

Many dog shows now hold agility as an exhibition. The ring is easy to find at the shows, as spectators can be four deep around the entire area. A great deal of enthusiasm emanates from all quarters—cheers from the spectators, barking from the dogs, and loud encouragement from the handlers. This is a fun sport, but not for the weak of heart!

COMPANION DOG

If you like to volunteer, it is a wonderful experience to take your Bull Terrier to a nursing home or hospital once a week for several hours. Senior citizens love to have a dog to visit with, and often your dog will bring a bit of companionship to someone who is either lonely or who may be somewhat detached from the world. You will not only be bringing happiness to someone else, but you will be keeping your dog busy—and we haven't even mentioned the discovery that volunteering helps to increase *your* longevity!

Raised dental tips on the surface of every Plaque Attacker™ bone help to combat plaque and tartar. Safe for aggressive chewers and ruggedly constructed to last, Plaque Attacker™ dental bones provide hours and hours of tooth-saving enjoyment.

The Bull Terrier is an energetic and intelligent dog and will be most happy when active.

Agility is just one of the many activities in which the Bull Terrier can demonstrate his athletic and competitive prowess.

SUGGESTED READING

JG 120
A New Owner's Guide
to Bull Terriers
Betty Desmond
160 pages, over 150 full-color photos

TS-249
Skin and Coat Care
for Your Dog
Dr. Lowell Ackerman, DVM
432 pages, over 300 full-color photos

TS-214
Owner's Guide to Dog Health
Dr. Lowell Ackerman, DVM
224 pages, over 190 full-color photos

TS-252
Dog Behavior and Training
Edited by Dr. Lowell Ackerman, DVM
292 pages, over 200 full-color photos

INDEX